The Teflon Don

The Untold Story of John Gotti, New York's Most Infamous Mob Boss

Lindsey T. Gordon

The Teflon Don

COPYRIGHT

TABLE OF CONTENTS

INTRODUCTION

The Rise of a Legend: Setting the Stage for John Gotti's Infamy

The story of John Gotti, later known as the "Teflon Don," is one that resonates with an almost mythical quality, marked by his swift rise from poverty in the Bronx to becoming one of the most feared and infamous mob bosses in America.

Gotti's early years set the stage for his later infamy; he grew up in a chaotic, impoverished household in New York City, where violence and crime were part of daily life. Born in 1940 to Italian immigrant parents, Gotti was one of 13 children, which made life financially challenging and often led him to fend for himself in the streets.

The Teflon Don

The allure of power and wealth found in organized crime proved irresistible to the young Gotti. He quickly fell in with local gangs, where he established a reputation for being fearless and calculating, a blend of charm and brutality that would follow him throughout his criminal career. By the time he was a teenager, Gotti was well-versed in the language of street violence, extortion, and theft, which attracted the attention of the Gambino crime family, one of New York's most powerful Mafia organizations.

As Gotti moved up the criminal ranks, his ambition and loyalty earned him the trust of high-ranking mob figures, who recognized in him the potential for something extraordinary. His capacity to remain unshaken by police pressure or legal threats set him apart from others in the underworld. Over time, he would evolve from a young, brash mobster into the "Dapper Don," a symbol of defiance and pride, revered by the public as much as he was feared by rivals. This rise from an impoverished boy in the Bronx to the most feared man in New York underlines the legendary status that John Gotti would come to hold.

The American Mafia: Understanding Organized Crime in 20th-Century New York

To understand John Gotti's rise to infamy, one must first comprehend the context of organized crime in 20th-century New York. The American Mafia, sometimes referred to as La Cosa Nostra (meaning "our thing" in

Italian), was a complex and powerful network of criminal families that had entrenched itself in various sectors of society. Emerging out of the early Italian immigrant communities in major American cities, the Mafia took root in New York and established its influence over various trades, including construction, shipping, gambling, and even politics.

The Five Families – Gambino, Lucchese, Genovese, Colombo, and Bonanno – each staked out territories and operated under a code of silence known as "Omertà," a sworn vow never to betray the secrets of the organization. These families carved up the city into territories, each with its hierarchy, its rules, and its bosses.

The Teflon Don

The Mafia acted both as a protector and enforcer in neighborhoods, often resolving disputes and providing economic opportunities through illicit channels. It created an ecosystem of organized crime that thrived under the radar, with tentacles reaching into unions, businesses, and political offices.

During the mid-20th century, the Mafia's influence reached its height, controlling billions in revenue and commanding respect and fear alike. For those born into poverty, like Gotti, the Mafia offered a path to power, wealth, and influence that seemed impossible through legitimate means.

This environment not only enabled Gotti's ascent but also fostered his disdain for the law and unyielding loyalty to the Mafia's principles. Gotti's eventual rise to power would signify both the peak of this organized crime era and, paradoxically, the beginning of its decline, as his visibility and defiance would draw unprecedented law enforcement attention to the Mafia's activities.

The Legacy of the Teflon Don: Gotti's Impact on the Criminal Underworld

John Gotti's reign as the head of the Gambino family left an indelible mark on the history of organized crime. His persona – from his immaculate, tailored suits to his unapologetic demeanor in the face of law enforcement – became the template for the "celebrity gangster."

The Teflon Don

Unlike his predecessors, who maintained a low profile and shunned public attention, Gotti embraced the spotlight, becoming as much a pop culture icon as a mob boss. His constant acquittals in high-profile cases earned him the nickname "The Teflon Don," and each courtroom victory further solidified his larger-than-life image.

Gotti's influence on the underworld was profound, not only for his brazen style but also for his disregard of Mafia traditions that prioritized secrecy and discretion. His actions attracted unprecedented media scrutiny and public fascination, which, while endearing him to the general public, increasingly put the Gambino family in the crosshairs of law enforcement.

The government's interest in Gotti forced the FBI to adopt new tactics, including the use of wiretaps and the cultivation of informants within the Mafia's ranks, ultimately leading to the most aggressive Mafia crackdown in American history.

When his former lieutenant, Sammy "The Bull" Gravano, turned state's witness, Gotti's empire began to crumble. His conviction in 1992 was a watershed moment that shattered the Mafia's grip on New York. Gotti's rise and fall became a cautionary tale for aspiring mobsters and a turning point for organized crime in America.

His flamboyant defiance of the law led to his downfall, but his legacy continues to resonate in popular culture and in the reshaped underworld, marking him as one of the last true mob bosses of his era and the one who forever changed the Mafia's place in American society.

CHAPTER ONE

The Making of a Mobster

John Gotti was born on October 27, 1940, in the Bronx, New York, one of 13 children in an Italian-American family. His parents, immigrants from Naples, Italy, struggled to make ends meet. John Sr., Gotti's father, found sporadic work as a day laborer, but his income was unreliable and meager, creating an environment of poverty and hardship for the large family.

The Gotti household was often marred by financial insecurity and tension, which fostered a resilience and toughness in young Gotti that would define his character for life. Early on, he learned that survival depended on strength, adaptability, and an ability to navigate difficult circumstances.

From a young age, Gotti's surroundings on the streets of Brooklyn's East New York neighborhood would shape his future. Growing up in a blue-collar, predominantly Italian-American area rife with petty crime, he was surrounded by boys and men who idolized the neighborhood mobsters.

For children like Gotti, these local gangsters embodied an alternative path to success, power, and respect—a stark contrast to the bleak life of poverty his father represented. His initial encounters with these figures fed his fascination with the world of organized crime, and he began to view the Mafia as a potential escape from the struggles of his family life.

In school, Gotti was unruly and quickly developed a reputation for defiance, eventually becoming known as a troublemaker. By age 12, he was involved in small-time thefts and fights, leading to frequent suspensions. Though his mother hoped for a different future, Gotti's attraction to the streets and the allure of quick money from illegal activities proved too strong. As he approached adolescence, his destiny seemed increasingly tied to the life of a mobster, setting him on a path that would one day lead him to the heights of the Gambino family.

Falling into Crime: Teenage Gotti's Introduction to the Underworld

As a teenager, John Gotti gravitated further into crime, spending more time with neighborhood gangs who dabbled in theft, robbery, and other petty offenses. By his mid-teens, Gotti was not only a frequent participant in local criminal activity but was also beginning to stand out for his fearlessness and willingness to do whatever was necessary to gain respect.

By 16, he was recruited into the Fulton-Rockaway Boys, a notorious street gang known for its connections to organized crime. In the gang, Gotti quickly established himself as a capable enforcer, gaining a reputation for being ruthless yet charismatic, a combination that made him both feared and respected.

These early years hardened Gotti, teaching him the unspoken codes and hierarchies that governed the underworld. He understood the importance of loyalty, strength, and fear in maintaining authority. During this period, he was involved in various crimes, from truck hijackings to extortion rackets. His activities began to catch the attention of local authorities, but he was skilled at avoiding major consequences, always covering his tracks well enough to evade serious punishment.

However, one incident nearly ended his career before it began—at age 14, while attempting to steal a cement mixer, he was severely injured when it fell and crushed his toes. The accident left him with a permanent limp, but it also marked his initiation into the life of a hardened criminal.

As he continued his illicit activities, Gotti attracted the attention of mobsters higher up in the Mafia's hierarchy. His commitment to the gang lifestyle and his ability to avoid legal consequences impressed the right people, and he began to move from street-level crime to more sophisticated operations.

By his late teens, Gotti was on the radar of key figures within the Gambino crime family, who saw promise in this young, ambitious enforcer. His connections with the Mafia deepened, paving the way for his entry into the world of organized crime, where he would soon become a key player.

The Gambino Family Connection: Joining One of New York's Most Notorious Crime Families

By the 1960s, Gotti had made a name for himself as a capable and loyal criminal within New York's Italian-American communities. His reputation for both fearlessness and reliability brought him to the attention of Carmine Fatico, a respected capo in the Gambino family, one of the Five Families that dominated organized crime in New York.

Fatico recognized Gotti's potential and brought him into his crew, officially integrating him into the ranks of the Gambino organization. It was a pivotal moment in Gotti's life, and his initiation into the Gambino family marked his entry into the sophisticated and lucrative world of organized crime.

As a member of the Gambino family, Gotti was given access to the family's various operations, which included gambling, loansharking, extortion, and truck hijacking—a specialty for which Gotti had a natural talent. Fatico placed him in charge of local hijackings, and Gotti excelled in orchestrating efficient, high-reward heists that further raised his profile within the family.

He quickly gained a reputation as a profitable asset, someone who could bring in significant money and enforce the family's interests with an iron fist. This responsibility also gave Gotti insight into the internal workings of the Mafia, allowing him to understand the complex relationships and power dynamics that governed the crime family.

Throughout his early years with the Gambino family, Gotti displayed an unwavering loyalty to Fatico and his fellow mobsters, adhering strictly to the *Omertà* code of silence. His success in these operations caught the attention of Carlo Gambino, the family's boss and one of the most powerful mobsters in New York.

Recognizing Gotti's potential, Gambino began to groom him for greater responsibility, putting him on the path to a high-ranking position within the organization. Under the guidance of Fatico and with Gambino's endorsement, Gotti learned how to wield power, intimidate rivals, and command respect, becoming an increasingly influential figure within the Mafia.

This period marked the consolidation of Gotti's identity as a "made man," bound by a lifelong commitment to the Gambino family. The family's code, loyalty, and ruthless tactics resonated deeply with Gotti, and he threw himself into his role with fervor.

Gotti's commitment to the family was further solidified when he carried out his first sanctioned hit under Fatico's orders, demonstrating his willingness to eliminate threats and proving that he had both the nerve and the brutality required of a true mobster. With this act, Gotti crossed a line, binding himself irrevocably to the life of organized crime and setting him on a path that would eventually lead him to the top of the Gambino empire.

In the years that followed, Gotti would climb through the ranks with unwavering ambition and strategic skill, becoming a trusted lieutenant and then a capo in his own right. These early years in the Bronx, his teenage initiation into crime, and his fateful connection to the Gambino family formed the foundation of a criminal career that would ultimately make him one of the most notorious mob bosses in American history.

CHAPTER TWO

Rising Through the Ranks

John Gotti's rise within the Gambino family began with a series of encounters that would define his path in the Mafia. The first of these was with Carmine Fatico, an influential capo within the Gambino organization who controlled a large portion of the family's operations in Queens and Brooklyn.

Fatico was a seasoned gangster, well-respected and trusted by Carlo Gambino himself, and he saw potential in the young Gotti. Fatico took Gotti under his wing, introducing him to the intricacies of Mafia life and offering him opportunities to prove his loyalty and skill.

Gotti's dedication and competence quickly set him apart from others. Fatico began involving Gotti in more complex operations, including hijackings, loansharking, and extortion, teaching him how to navigate the Mafia's code of conduct and the delicate power dynamics that governed the family.

As Gotti worked under Fatico, he also encountered other key figures in the Gambino family, including Aniello Dellacroce, a powerful underboss known for his ruthless enforcement and unwavering loyalty to the Gambino family. Dellacroce was feared and respected throughout the Mafia for his cold, calculating nature and ability to command respect through intimidation alone.

The Teflon Don

For Gotti, Dellacroce became a powerful mentor and a figure of admiration. Dellacroce recognized Gotti's potential and took a liking to the young mobster, whose fearlessness and loyalty mirrored his own. In Dellacroce, Gotti found a role model who epitomized the ideals of the Mafia—strength, loyalty, and an unyielding adherence to the code of "Omertà."

This mentorship would become crucial in Gotti's rise, as Dellacroce would eventually endorse him for higher positions within the Gambino hierarchy. Through these relationships, Gotti's loyalty to the Gambino family deepened, and he became further entrenched in the world of organized crime, laying the foundation for his eventual rise to power.

An Enforcer's Loyalty: Gotti's Role as a Hitman and Enforcer

Under Carmine Fatico's guidance, Gotti assumed the role of an enforcer for the Gambino family, a position that required him to be both a protector and a punisher. As an enforcer, Gotti was responsible for carrying out orders against those who threatened the family's interests or dared to challenge its authority.

His duties ranged from collecting debts and enforcing the family's rules to intimidating or eliminating rivals and informants. This role demanded a mix of brutal efficiency and unshakeable loyalty, both of which Gotti possessed in abundance.

One of Gotti's early assignments was to oversee the family's hijacking operations, which proved to be both profitable and dangerous. Truck hijacking was a lucrative business, allowing the Gambino family to seize valuable goods and sell them on the black market. Gotti quickly showed his talent for organizing these operations, coordinating teams, and executing heists with precision.

His success in hijackings not only earned the family significant profits but also bolstered his reputation within the organization. He became known as a reliable earner and an effective enforcer, willing to do whatever was necessary to safeguard the family's interests.

Beyond hijackings, Gotti was involved in more violent assignments, often carrying out hits on behalf of the Gambino family. His first sanctioned killing marked a turning point in his career. Tasked with eliminating a traitor who had been cooperating with the authorities, Gotti demonstrated his willingness to follow orders without hesitation, solidifying his reputation as a trusted hitman.

His role as an enforcer required a level of ruthlessness that few could match, and his ability to carry out these violent tasks with cold precision impressed his superiors, including Aniello Dellacroce.

Gotti's work as an enforcer forged a bond of trust between him and Dellacroce, who saw in him a protégé capable of enforcing the family's rule with the same relentless commitment that Dellacroce himself embodied. Over time, Gotti became not only a feared enforcer but also a respected figure within the Gambino family, seen by many as a future leader. His role as a hitman and enforcer was essential to his rise, demonstrating both his loyalty and his capability, qualities that would ultimately lead to greater opportunities within the family's ranks.

The Capo Promotion: Ascending to Capo and Gaining Influence in the Family

As Gotti's reputation grew, so did his responsibilities. His success as an enforcer and earner made him a valuable asset to the Gambino family, and in the early 1970s, he received a significant promotion: he was made a capo, or captain, a position of substantial authority within the Mafia. A capo controlled a crew of soldiers and associates, managing their activities, resolving conflicts, and overseeing various revenue-generating operations. For Gotti, this promotion was a monumental step, one that solidified his status as a key player in the Gambino hierarchy.

In his new role, Gotti was given control over a crew based in Queens, where he managed a range of illicit activities, including gambling, loansharking, and extortion. His crew brought in substantial profits, further enhancing his standing within the family. As capo, Gotti had a reputation for being both demanding and generous; he expected loyalty and discipline from his men, but he also rewarded them well, ensuring their loyalty through both fear and financial incentive. This leadership style made him popular among his crew and reinforced his reputation as a capable and respected leader.

Gotti's promotion also brought him closer to the family's inner circle, allowing him to participate in high-level meetings and decisions that shaped the Gambino family's operations. He now had direct access to influential figures such as Carlo Gambino and Aniello Dellacroce, both of whom respected his abilities and saw him as a rising star within the organization. Gotti's loyalty to Dellacroce, in particular, remained steadfast, and he considered him not only a mentor but also a father figure. This bond proved instrumental as tensions began to emerge within the Gambino family over the future leadership of the organization.

As capo, Gotti faced new challenges and opportunities, navigating the political intrigues and rivalries that characterized the upper echelons of the Mafia. He became involved in disputes with other families and internal conflicts, always striving to protect his crew and expand his influence.

His ambition was clear, and he was not content to remain a capo indefinitely; he had his sights set on the highest ranks of the organization. This ambition, combined with his skills as a leader and enforcer, would eventually propel him toward his ultimate goal: becoming the boss of the Gambino family.

Gotti's ascension to capo marked the beginning of his climb to the top of the Gambino family. His ability to lead, his unwavering loyalty, and his willingness to enforce the family's rules with an iron hand made him one of the most formidable figures in the organization. This promotion was not only a testament to his talents but also a stepping stone on his journey to become one of the most infamous mob bosses in American history, setting the stage for the dramatic events that would follow.

CHAPTER THREE

The Assassination of Paul Castellano

By the early 1980s, John Gotti was already a powerful figure within the Gambino family, yet he was restless. He harbored ambitions of taking full control of the organization, driven by his vision of a more aggressive and public-facing approach that contrasted sharply with the leadership style of then-boss Paul Castellano.

Castellano had risen to power after the death of the infamous Carlo Gambino and had continued to lead the family with a more business-like, low-profile demeanor, preferring diplomacy over open violence and strongly emphasizing secrecy. However, Castellano's leadership style and policies didn't sit well with Gotti and others within the organization who craved a more assertive approach.

Several factors fed Gotti's dissatisfaction with Castellano's leadership. First, Castellano had alienated many within the family by focusing more on white-collar crime, including union racketeering and construction industry deals, while neglecting the traditional street-level operations that were the bread and butter for men like Gotti.

Additionally, Castellano's emphasis on distancing the family from street violence clashed with Gotti's preference for intimidation and force. Furthermore, Gotti resented Castellano's arrogance and the fact that Castellano often saw himself as above other family members.

This tension reached a breaking point when Castellano made the controversial decision to promote his driver and protégé, Thomas Bilotti, over more senior and experienced captains, intensifying the resentment among the Gambino ranks.

However, the catalyst for Gotti's desire to eliminate Castellano came with Castellano's legal troubles. By 1984, Castellano faced a slew of charges, including racketeering, which brought a new level of scrutiny from law enforcement. Gotti feared that if Castellano were convicted, he might strike a deal with authorities to save himself, potentially jeopardizing the entire family.

This paranoia, coupled with Gotti's long-standing ambition, led him to begin conspiring with other disaffected members of the family to remove Castellano and seize control.

Gotti carefully cultivated support from influential members of the Gambino family, especially those who shared his frustrations with Castellano's leadership. He turned to powerful allies, including his loyal underboss, Sammy "The Bull" Gravano, a ruthless and highly influential figure whose support would prove invaluable.

With Gravano and other disgruntled captains behind him, Gotti laid the groundwork for a bold and dangerous plan: assassinate Paul Castellano and assume leadership of the Gambino family. It was a high-stakes scheme that, if successful, would catapult him to the top of New York's criminal hierarchy—but if it failed, it would almost certainly lead to his death.

A Christmas Coup: The Hit on Castellano Outside Sparks Steakhouse

On December 16, 1985, Gotti and his allies executed one of the most audacious and high-profile mob hits in modern history. Paul Castellano and his newly appointed underboss, Thomas Bilotti, were scheduled to dine at Sparks Steakhouse, a popular Midtown Manhattan restaurant. Gotti, along with Sammy Gravano and other co-conspirators, meticulously planned every detail of the assassination to ensure that Castellano would be eliminated swiftly and publicly, sending a powerful message to both the Gambino family and the broader Mafia community.

That evening, Gotti and Gravano waited in a car near Sparks Steakhouse, observing the scene while a team of four hitmen took their positions. The plan was for Castellano's car to pull up in front of the restaurant, where the gunmen would approach and eliminate both Castellano and Bilotti. As Castellano's car arrived and the men stepped out, the hitmen approached quickly and, in a calculated and coordinated attack, opened fire on Castellano and Bilotti.

Both men were killed instantly, lying dead on the sidewalk in a bloody spectacle that shocked bystanders and the media alike. The brazen nature of the assassination, occurring in broad daylight in Midtown

Manhattan, marked a stark departure from the Mafia's traditional approach to violence, which usually aimed to avoid public exposure.

The murder of Castellano sent shockwaves throughout the underworld and signaled a changing of the guard within the Gambino family. For Gotti, the hit was both a triumph and a public declaration of his rise to power. The brutal public assassination broke longstanding Mafia protocols, which favored discretion and limited violence, but it also demonstrated Gotti's audacity and absolute willingness to break the rules to achieve his ambitions.

Gotti had gambled his life on this bold move, knowing that failure would almost certainly lead to retaliation from loyalists within the family or rival mob factions. Yet his gamble had paid off; Castellano was dead, and Gotti had cleared the path to assume leadership of the Gambino family.

Becoming Boss: Gotti's Coronation as Head of the Gambino Family

Following Castellano's assassination, Gotti moved swiftly to consolidate his control over the Gambino family. The day after the hit, Gotti summoned key members of the family to discuss the new hierarchy. With Castellano gone and no immediate challenges to his authority, Gotti declared himself the new boss, an act that effectively reshaped the Gambino family and cemented his place at the top of New York's Mafia.

The Teflon Don

The ascension of Gotti as boss marked a turning point in Mafia history. Traditionally, the transition of power within a crime family would be handled discreetly, but Gotti's rise was anything but subtle. His ascent was accompanied by an unprecedented level of media coverage and public attention, which Gotti welcomed.

Unlike Castellano, who preferred to stay in the shadows, Gotti reveled in the spotlight, quickly earning the moniker "The Dapper Don" due to his flamboyant style, expensive suits, and habit of smiling for reporters. Gotti's public persona marked a radical departure from previous bosses who had avoided media attention, understanding that exposure brought scrutiny. For Gotti, however, the attention reinforced his image as an invincible and charismatic leader who could outsmart the system.

Gotti's leadership style combined charm with a ruthless streak. As boss, he emphasized loyalty and demanded respect from his subordinates, rewarding those who supported him and quickly eliminating anyone who showed signs of disloyalty. He maintained a close circle of trusted associates, with Sammy Gravano serving as his underboss and right-hand man.

Together, Gotti and Gravano reshaped the family's operations, increasing involvement in narcotics, loansharking, and other high-stakes rackets that brought in millions of dollars. Gotti also worked to strengthen the Gambino family's influence over the New York Mafia Commission, positioning himself as a powerful figure in the wider underworld.

While Gotti's public visibility boosted his reputation, it also attracted increased law enforcement attention. His open defiance of the FBI and his "untouchable" attitude led authorities to intensify their efforts to bring him down. Under Gotti, the Gambino family thrived, but the increased scrutiny would prove to be both a boon and a curse. Law enforcement's growing focus on Gotti eventually led to the use of wiretaps, undercover informants, and unprecedented surveillance, all aimed at dismantling his empire.

Despite these challenges, Gotti's coronation as head of the Gambino family marked the peak of his criminal career. He ruled with a combination of charisma, intimidation, and strategic acumen, cementing his legacy as one of the most infamous mob bosses in history. However, his desire for fame and notoriety would ultimately set the stage for his downfall.

CHAPTER FOUR

The Rise of the Teflon Don

John Gotti's entanglement with law enforcement began early in his criminal career, reflecting both his audacious attitude and his growing prominence in the underworld. His initial run-ins with the law were relatively minor compared to the high-profile cases he would face in later years, but they offered him his first taste of the cat-and-mouse game that would define his relationship with authorities.

As a young enforcer and capo in the Gambino family, Gotti was often involved in hijackings, assaults, and extortion schemes—crimes that frequently drew the attention of the police. While he was arrested several times, he managed to avoid lengthy prison sentences, which emboldened him and bolstered his reputation as a man who was "untouchable."

One of Gotti's earliest significant encounters with the law occurred in 1968, when he was arrested for hijacking trucks at Kennedy Airport. Alongside his associates, Gotti orchestrated a lucrative operation that involved seizing goods from transport trucks and reselling them on the black market. Though he was ultimately sentenced to three years in prison for this crime, Gotti's brief incarceration did little to discourage his ambitions. On the contrary, he returned to the streets with a stronger sense of his own resilience and an even deeper loyalty to the Gambino family.

Over the years, Gotti became increasingly adept at avoiding convictions, a skill that would serve him well as his profile rose. He learned how to work the system, relying on bribes, intimidation, and witness tampering to protect himself and ensure that those who might testify against him were either silenced or persuaded to withdraw their statements.

His early legal battles taught him not only the importance of cultivating loyalty but also how to manipulate both the criminal and judicial systems to his advantage. With each case he managed to beat, his aura of invincibility grew, laying the foundation for the public persona that would eventually earn him the nickname "The Teflon Don."

Acquittals and the Media: How Gotti Built His "Teflon Don" Persona

As John Gotti climbed the ranks of the Gambino family, he became a high-value target for law enforcement agencies determined to bring him down. However, Gotti's remarkable success in court began to draw public attention and cement his reputation as a mobster who was virtually immune to prosecution.

Despite the FBI's growing surveillance efforts, Gotti repeatedly evaded convictions, a feat that baffled authorities and captivated the public. It was during this period that he began to build the persona that would define him in the media: a charismatic, invincible gangster whose crimes seemed to slide off him like water on Teflon.

The Teflon Don

The term "Teflon Don" was coined in the 1980s after Gotti was acquitted in a series of high-profile trials. One of the most notable cases involved a 1986 federal racketeering charge, in which Gotti faced accusations of heading an extensive criminal enterprise. The trial, however, ended in Gotti's favor after several key witnesses either refused to testify or delivered testimony that appeared weak and unreliable.

Gotti's legal team, led by the formidable defense attorney Bruce Cutler, argued that the charges were part of a conspiracy by the government to bring down an innocent man. The defense strategy succeeded in creating doubt, and once again, Gotti walked free.

The Teflon Don

The press coverage surrounding Gotti's acquittals only fed the myth of the "Teflon Don." Media outlets began to paint Gotti as a larger-than-life figure, a man who defied both the law and the odds with remarkable consistency. Reporters and photographers eagerly followed his court appearances, where Gotti's flashy attire, confident demeanor, and easy smile contrasted sharply with the typical image of a mob boss.

This persona—cool, composed, and always one step ahead of the law—resonated with the public, who were both fascinated and horrified by his apparent invincibility. Gotti's repeated successes in court became symbolic of his power over the justice system, reinforcing the perception that he was untouchable.

Gotti's lawyer, Bruce Cutler, played a crucial role in shaping this public image, often delivering passionate defenses that cast Gotti as a victim of government persecution rather than a hardened criminal. Cutler's spirited courtroom performances, combined with Gotti's undeniable charisma, transformed each trial into a spectacle that captivated viewers nationwide. The press embraced the "Teflon Don" moniker, and Gotti's image as a celebrity gangster took on a life of its own, overshadowing the brutal reality of his criminal empire.

The Teflon Don

The Celebrity Mob Boss: Gotti's Rise to Public Fame and Infamy

John Gotti's ascent as a media icon marked a new era for organized crime in America, as he became perhaps the first mob boss to fully embrace the role of a public figure. Unlike previous Mafia leaders who operated in the shadows, Gotti seemed to thrive on the attention.

He dressed in tailored suits, attended high-profile social events, and moved with an entourage that emphasized his status. His flair for style earned him the additional nickname "The Dapper Don," and his popularity with the media transformed him into a kind of anti-hero. For many Americans, he embodied both the allure and the danger of the Mafia lifestyle.

Gotti's media presence extended beyond the courtroom. Reporters and photographers would often catch glimpses of him at clubs, restaurants, and even charitable events, where he mingled with celebrities, politicians, and other high-profile figures. He became a fixture of New York's social scene, flaunting his wealth and charisma in a way that attracted admirers and further mystified his detractors.

For some members of the public, Gotti's defiance of the authorities became an almost admirable quality. Here was a man who, despite the FBI's best efforts, continued to live freely, laughing in the face of the law. His appeal as a "celebrity mob boss" was unprecedented, captivating Americans who watched his saga unfold in newspapers and on television.

However, Gotti's fame was a double-edged sword. While it increased his influence and gave him a certain level of public support, it also intensified the resolve of law enforcement to bring him down. FBI agents and federal prosecutors were both frustrated and embarrassed by their inability to secure a conviction against him, which only motivated them to dig deeper into his activities.

As his celebrity grew, so did the scrutiny, with authorities determined to find the evidence that would finally make charges stick. The FBI expanded its surveillance operations, deploying a network of informants, wiretaps, and undercover agents to gather intelligence on Gotti's organization and criminal dealings.

Gotti's desire for fame ultimately led him to make critical mistakes that would contribute to his downfall. His high-profile lifestyle attracted more attention than was prudent for a man in his line of work, making him a symbol of the Mafia's resilience but also exposing his every move.

He was no longer just another mob boss; he had become a larger-than-life figure whose exploits were monitored by law enforcement and the public alike. This scrutiny, coupled with his unwillingness to retreat from the spotlight, would eventually erode his Teflon-like reputation and lead to his eventual capture and conviction.

The Teflon Don

In the end, John Gotti's rise as the "Teflon Don" exemplified the allure and the perils of public infamy. His image as a stylish, invincible crime lord became an iconic part of New York City's lore, capturing the fascination of the American public and setting a new precedent for how organized crime was perceived.

Gotti's flamboyance and charisma ensured that he would be remembered as one of the most famous mobsters of his era, but his desire for fame and public recognition ultimately undermined his efforts to avoid prosecution. As Gotti's fame grew, so did the determination of law enforcement to bring him down, setting the stage for a dramatic clash that would define the later years of his life and legacy.

CHAPTER FIVE

The Empire Expands

After assuming power as head of the Gambino crime family, John Gotti set about solidifying and expanding the family's control over a range of lucrative operations. His empire thrived on a mix of traditional and evolving criminal enterprises, with Gotti expanding operations in areas like drug trafficking, gambling, and extortion.

Despite the Mafia's historical reluctance to embrace the narcotics trade due to the heightened risk of federal prosecution, Gotti saw the enormous profits drugs could generate and allowed certain factions of the family to continue their involvement in drug distribution, albeit discreetly.

One of Gotti's key strategies was to increase control over street-level drug trade in New York's outer boroughs, including Queens, Brooklyn, and the Bronx. Gotti developed partnerships with local drug dealers who were allowed to operate under the Gambino family's protection as long as they paid a percentage of their earnings.

This arrangement benefited both parties: dealers gained security and credibility under the Gambino name, while Gotti profited without being directly involved in the day-to-day operations. This layer of separation allowed Gotti to insulate himself from legal repercussions while still reaping the rewards of the drug trade.

Gotti also strengthened the family's hold on illegal gambling, which had always been a reliable source of income for the Mafia. Bookmaking, sports betting, and high-stakes card games flourished under Gotti's reign, with operations spanning across bars, nightclubs, and private clubs.

Gotti set up networks of bookmakers who operated under strict orders, ensuring a steady flow of cash without drawing unnecessary attention. In addition to traditional gambling, the family expanded into video poker and slot machines in bars and social clubs, particularly in neighborhoods where they could operate with minimal interference from authorities.

Extortion, another cornerstone of Gotti's empire, became increasingly sophisticated under his leadership. Gotti implemented a systematic approach to extorting small businesses, restaurants, construction companies, and unions across New York. Business owners paid "protection" money in exchange for assurances that the Gambino family would protect their businesses from theft, arson, or harassment.

This system of control extended to construction sites and labor unions, where Gotti's men ensured contracts were awarded to businesses loyal to the family. By securing influence over unions, particularly in construction, Gotti strengthened his control over some of New York's most lucrative industries. His mastery over these rackets allowed him to create a vast income stream that further solidified the Gambino family's financial power.

Internal Loyalty and Betrayal: Managing Power and the Code of Silence

As the boss of the Gambino family, Gotti faced the dual challenge of fostering loyalty while protecting himself from betrayal—a constant threat within the cutthroat world of organized crime. The Mafia's code of omertà, or silence, was central to maintaining the secrecy and integrity of the family's operations.

Gotti was keenly aware of the importance of this code and took extreme measures to ensure that it was respected by his men. He cultivated a culture of loyalty and fear, rewarding those who served him faithfully while swiftly dealing with anyone who showed signs of disloyalty.

Gotti's close relationship with his underboss, Sammy "The Bull" Gravano, became one of his most significant alliances. Gravano was not only fiercely loyal but also ruthless and efficient—a crucial asset for Gotti's leadership. Gravano managed many of the family's operations, allowing Gotti to focus on broader strategic moves.

However, even this alliance was founded on the volatile understanding that loyalty in the Mafia was often conditional and could be fractured if circumstances changed. To prevent betrayal, Gotti developed a strict vetting process for those he allowed into his inner circle, ensuring that only the most trustworthy and loyal individuals were granted access to critical information.

Nonetheless, Gotti's leadership style had its pitfalls. His highly public profile and frequent legal battles created friction within the family, with some members questioning the wisdom of his approach. While Gotti was respected and feared, his insistence on a flashy, high-profile lifestyle exposed the organization to increased law enforcement attention.

This brought tension to the surface, as some felt that Gotti's fame was undermining the family's traditional values of discretion. To keep dissent in check, Gotti employed a blend of charm and intimidation, holding regular meetings to gauge loyalty and eliminate any potential threats. Associates who expressed discontent or hesitancy were often removed from their positions—or worse.

Despite his efforts to enforce loyalty, Gotti could not entirely prevent betrayal. The internal conflicts within the family eventually came to a head as cracks in the structure appeared. Under his rule, more family members began cooperating with law enforcement, breaking the sacred omertà. These defections would ultimately prove to be Gotti's undoing, as government witnesses provided damning testimony that eroded the carefully built walls of secrecy surrounding his empire.

Ruling the Gambino Family with an Iron Fist: Gotti's Ruthless Command

John Gotti's leadership style was defined by a unique combination of charisma and ruthlessness, traits that allowed him to command the respect and fear of his underlings while effectively managing one of the most powerful Mafia families in New York. His approach to leadership was both strategic and brutal, and he made it clear that he would tolerate no challenges to his authority. Those who crossed him faced severe consequences, as Gotti used violence and intimidation to maintain absolute control over the Gambino family.

Gotti's reputation as a ruthless leader was solidified by his willingness to eliminate anyone who threatened his position. Unlike his predecessor, Paul Castellano, who avoided violence whenever possible, Gotti did not hesitate to order hits on family members and associates who were suspected of disloyalty. His iron-fisted rule became a hallmark of his reign, with numerous cases of individuals who met untimely ends after falling out of favor.

Under Gotti, the family's hitmen operated with deadly efficiency, and even the slightest indication of disloyalty could result in swift and fatal punishment. This environment of fear ensured that few dared to defy him, as the consequences were clear and often lethal.

One of the key methods Gotti used to enforce his power was the strategic use of public displays of violence. By making an example out of traitors or enemies, he sent a message not only to his own family but also to other Mafia organizations. In one high-profile case, a Gambino soldier suspected of cooperating with law enforcement was brutally murdered, his body left in a public place as a warning to others. These acts of intimidation underscored Gotti's ruthless approach to power, making it clear that anyone who betrayed the family would pay the ultimate price.

Yet, Gotti's leadership was not solely based on fear. He had an innate ability to inspire loyalty among those who served him faithfully. His charm, sense of loyalty to his men, and his reputation as a "man of the people" within the Mafia allowed him to attract and retain loyal followers. Gotti maintained a small but trusted inner circle, who were rewarded with wealth and privileges in return for their service and loyalty.

To those who proved their loyalty, Gotti could be remarkably generous, ensuring that they shared in the family's profits and were treated with respect. This balancing act of reward and punishment created a powerful, albeit volatile, hierarchy within the Gambino family.

Under Gotti's iron rule, the Gambino family flourished financially but faced growing challenges. His uncompromising leadership style protected him from internal threats, but his high-profile persona increasingly drew the attention of law enforcement. His empire expanded as he solidified control over various criminal enterprises, but Gotti's methods also created underlying tensions that would eventually lead to significant fractures within his organization.

The paradox of Gotti's reign was that, while his ruthlessness kept him safe from internal threats, his defiance of law enforcement and the Mafia's traditional values ultimately made him more vulnerable to external forces.

In the end, Gotti's command over the Gambino family showcased his formidable leadership and capacity for ruthlessness. His iron-fisted rule created an environment of fear and loyalty, ensuring his dominance but also isolating him from the support he would need when the tides turned against him. The fear he inspired helped him maintain control, but it also left him without allies when he needed them most, setting the stage for the dramatic unraveling of his empire.

CHAPTER SIX

Inside the FBI's Investigation

As John Gotti's public persona grew more flamboyant, the FBI intensified its efforts to bring him to justice. His nickname, the "Teflon Don," was not a source of amusement within law enforcement circles, but a frustration and a challenge. Gotti's repeated court victories, thanks in part to intimidation of witnesses and strong defense tactics, made him seem untouchable, and this only spurred the FBI to increase its surveillance efforts.

They were determined to find concrete evidence that could finally convict him, and in the mid-1980s, the FBI launched an expansive and highly focused investigation targeting Gotti and the Gambino family.

Initially, the FBI's surveillance involved tracking Gotti's movements, photographing him as he conducted day-to-day activities and frequently visiting known Gambino family haunts in New York. Agents observed him at social clubs, particularly the Ravenite Social Club, which was a popular gathering spot for Gotti and his associates in Little Italy.

This surveillance yielded a wealth of information about Gotti's routines, his close associates, and his apparent indifference to the risks associated with being seen in public. Despite the ever-present FBI surveillance, Gotti continued to conduct family business with a brazen confidence, seemingly unfazed by the agents tailing him.

Recognizing that mere observation would not be enough to dismantle Gotti's operation, the FBI decided to deploy more sophisticated methods. The agency began tapping the phones of known associates and planting undercover agents in bars and businesses that were frequented by the Gambino family. These initial surveillance efforts, while yielding minimal direct evidence, provided invaluable insights into the inner workings of Gotti's organization.

They were able to observe the structure of the Gambino family, the hierarchy of his trusted associates, and the ways in which orders were passed down the chain of command without implicating Gotti directly.

The FBI's persistence in surveillance gradually chipped away at the wall of secrecy that had previously protected Gotti and his criminal empire.

Bugging the Ravenite Social Club: Key Recordings That Uncovered Gotti's Activities

The FBI's investigation took a decisive turn when agents succeeded in planting recording devices within the Ravenite Social Club. This was a bold and risky move; the Ravenite was not only Gotti's favored meeting place but also a symbol of his confidence and defiance toward law enforcement.

Under normal circumstances, the Ravenite was heavily guarded, and Mafia members were vigilant about the possibility of electronic surveillance. To avoid suspicion, Gotti and his men regularly scanned the club for hidden devices and often spoke in coded language or used gestures to communicate.

To overcome these obstacles, FBI agents orchestrated a meticulous plan to infiltrate the Ravenite. Knowing they couldn't simply walk into the club and plant a bug, they waited for a rare opportunity when Gotti and his associates were away from the premises. Undercover agents disguised as utility workers entered the building under the pretense of performing routine maintenance, allowing them to install sophisticated listening devices in several locations.

The agents placed these bugs in the walls and ceilings of the club, ensuring that key conversations between Gotti and his captains could be recorded without raising suspicion. This move marked a turning point in the investigation, as these recordings would eventually reveal the inner workings of Gotti's criminal activities.

The recordings captured at the Ravenite proved invaluable to the FBI. They provided clear evidence of Gotti's direct involvement in criminal enterprises and documented his role in orchestrating various illegal activities. In these conversations, Gotti discussed murders, extortion schemes, and the distribution of family profits, providing the FBI with irrefutable proof of his criminal leadership.

One particularly damning recording featured Gotti angrily criticizing his underboss, Sammy "The Bull" Gravano, and discussing past murders he had authorized, including the hit on Paul Castellano. These recordings would later serve as the foundation of the government's case against Gotti, revealing his role as the mastermind behind the Gambino family's operations and making it impossible for him to distance himself from the crimes committed under his orders.

The impact of these recordings was profound. For years, Gotti had managed to avoid conviction by relying on indirect communication, coded language, and intimidation to keep witnesses silent. However, the FBI's success in capturing these unguarded moments at the Ravenite rendered those strategies ineffective.

The recordings gave the FBI a rare glimpse into the unfiltered dynamics of the Gambino family and provided a direct link between Gotti and the crimes committed by his organization. These tapes shattered the image of the "Teflon Don" and exposed the ruthless reality of his leadership, setting the stage for the FBI's next steps in bringing Gotti to justice.

Cracking the Code: Investigators Decipher Gotti's Network

With the recordings from the Ravenite Social Club in hand, the FBI turned its attention to deciphering the complex web of relationships and communications within

Gotti's criminal empire. The Gambino family operated under a strict hierarchy, with orders passed down through trusted captains and soldiers to minimize exposure for the top leadership. Gotti rarely handled illegal transactions directly, relying instead on a network of intermediaries to shield him from prosecution. To dismantle this structure, the FBI needed to unravel the intricate codes, aliases, and signals that Gotti's associates used to conduct business.

The FBI established a team of analysts to study the recorded conversations, identifying patterns in speech, gestures, and coded references that had previously eluded investigators. These analysts worked closely with informants and former Mafia members who provided critical insights into the language and customs of the Gambino family.

Through this process, the FBI began to map out Gotti's criminal network, identifying the roles and responsibilities of various associates and decoding the phrases they used to discuss illegal activities without incriminating themselves. Terms like "taking care of business" were revealed to mean organizing hits, while seemingly innocent references to "work" often implied extortion or other criminal activities.

One of the most challenging aspects of cracking the code was understanding Gotti's role as a symbolic and practical leader. Gotti's public persona as a Mafia "celebrity" was a calculated façade that allowed him to conduct business while diverting attention away from the family's deeper criminal operations.

To the public, he was "The Dapper Don," but within his organization, he was a decisive and brutal leader, carefully balancing relationships with subordinates to maintain control. The FBI's analysts learned that Gotti often used his public image as a diversion tactic, drawing attention to his charisma and style while conducting his real business behind closed doors.

As the investigation progressed, the FBI also discovered how Gotti managed internal conflicts and maintained control over his subordinates. The tapes revealed a careful mix of rewards for loyalty and severe consequences for dissent. Gotti's reputation for dealing harshly with traitors was well-known, but the recordings illuminated the personal methods he used to foster loyalty and respect among his men.

His leadership was a combination of calculated charm and brutality, both inspiring loyalty and instilling fear in his underlings. This information was instrumental in the FBI's strategy, as it allowed agents to predict Gotti's moves and exploit divisions within the family.

Ultimately, the FBI's efforts to decipher Gotti's network and language provided the key to understanding how the Gambino family operated under his command. By gaining insights into the complex hierarchy and communications structure, investigators could anticipate Gotti's next moves and target his most vulnerable associates.

This approach allowed the FBI to build a case that would withstand the legal challenges Gotti had previously used to evade prosecution. Armed with recordings, decoded language, and a comprehensive understanding of the Gambino family's inner workings, the FBI was finally prepared to move forward with charges that would challenge the untouchable status of the "Teflon Don" and bring his criminal empire to the brink of collapse.

CHAPTER SEVEN

Sammy "The Bull" Gravano Turns

Sammy "The Bull" Gravano was one of the most feared and respected figures within the Gambino crime family. Known for his loyalty, cunning, and willingness to carry out brutal acts of violence, Gravano rose through the ranks as a trusted enforcer and eventually became John Gotti's right-hand man.

Gravano's reputation as a steadfast, loyal mobster was deeply ingrained within the Mafia world, making his later decision to turn against Gotti all the more shocking. To understand the weight of Gravano's betrayal, it is essential to examine the complex, layered relationship he shared with Gotti—a bond marked by mutual respect, fear, and a shared commitment to the Mafia's codes, yet one that was ultimately doomed by ambition and survival instincts.

Gotti and Gravano's relationship was defined by complementary strengths and a mutual dependence. While Gotti was the charismatic, high-profile boss who commanded attention with his public persona, Gravano operated behind the scenes as the enforcer and strategist, managing the family's business interests and enforcing discipline among its members.

Gotti relied on Gravano's loyalty and expertise to maintain control over the family, and Gravano admired Gotti's leadership and charisma, viewing him as a powerful figure worthy of respect. Together, they formed a partnership that allowed the Gambino family to thrive during Gotti's reign, and Gravano's presence gave Gotti a level of security within his organization, knowing he had a fierce ally by his side.

However, their partnership was not without its tensions. Gravano's own ambitions and increasing frustration with Gotti's leadership style simmered beneath the surface. While Gravano had initially admired Gotti's flair and boldness, he began to question the wisdom of Gotti's high-profile approach. Gotti's penchant for public appearances and media attention contrasted sharply with Gravano's belief in operating discreetly—a principle that had historically helped the Mafia avoid detection.

As Gotti continued to court media attention, Gravano worried that the heightened visibility would bring unwanted scrutiny to the Gambino family, making it increasingly difficult for them to operate in the shadows. This fundamental difference in philosophy planted the seeds of doubt in Gravano, and over time, this tension would play a crucial role in his decision to betray the boss he once revered.

Gravano's frustrations were compounded by Gotti's tendency to blame others for problems within the family. While Gravano was fiercely loyal, he began to feel alienated by Gotti's repeated criticisms of his methods and decisions. In private conversations—many of which were captured by the FBI's hidden microphones at the Ravenite Social Club—Gotti often disparaged Gravano, blaming him for various mishaps and even discussing Gravano's role in murders in a way that suggested a lack of respect for the code of silence.

These criticisms wounded Gravano's pride and fueled his growing resentment. Gotti's unwillingness to shoulder responsibility, coupled with his public criticisms of Gravano, pushed the underboss closer to a breaking point, setting the stage for the unprecedented betrayal that would ultimately dismantle Gotti's empire.

A Fateful Decision: Gravano's Defection to the Government

Gravano's decision to defect to the government remains one of the most consequential moments in the history of organized crime in the United States. For a high-ranking Mafia member, cooperating with law enforcement was almost unthinkable—a direct violation of omertà, the Mafia's sacred code of silence.

However, by 1991, Gravano found himself in an impossible position, caught between loyalty to Gotti and a desire for self-preservation. Facing life imprisonment and disillusioned by Gotti's leadership, Gravano made the fateful decision to turn against the man he had once admired and serve as a government witness.

The FBI's relentless pursuit of the Gambino family had finally yielded results, and both Gotti and Gravano were facing serious charges, including racketeering and murder. The turning point for Gravano came when he learned of Gotti's taped conversations at the Ravenite Social Club, in which Gotti not only criticized Gravano but also discussed their involvement in numerous murders.

These recordings were damning, and Gravano realized that Gotti's willingness to implicate him suggested a betrayal of their supposed bond. He understood that if convicted alongside Gotti, he would likely face life in prison, with little hope of ever regaining his freedom. For Gravano, the choice became one of loyalty versus survival.

The FBI, recognizing the potential impact of Gravano's testimony, approached him with a deal that would eventually lead to Gotti's downfall. After weeks of negotiations and soul-searching, Gravano agreed to cooperate with the government, marking a seismic shift in Mafia culture. His defection was a historic moment—the underboss of one of the most powerful crime families in America was now an informant, willing to testify against his boss and reveal the inner workings of the Gambino family.

This decision was not made lightly; Gravano grappled with the emotional and ethical implications of betraying Gotti and violating the Mafia's core principles. Yet, his resentment toward Gotti and the survival instincts that had long served him in the underworld ultimately outweighed his sense of loyalty.

In defecting, Gravano provided federal prosecutors with a treasure trove of information. He detailed the operations of the Gambino family, outlined the family's hierarchy, and, most crucially, provided firsthand accounts of Gotti's involvement in multiple murders, including the plot to kill former boss Paul Castellano.

Gravano's testimony exposed the dark, violent reality behind Gotti's glamorous image and dismantled the myth of the "Teflon Don" once and for all. With Gravano's cooperation, the government had the evidence it needed to secure a conviction that would finally bring an end to Gotti's reign.

A Betrayal of Loyalty: The Impact of Gravano's Testimony on Gotti's Fate

Gravano's testimony was devastating for Gotti. In a series of damning revelations, Gravano described in meticulous detail the Gambino family's criminal activities, from racketeering and extortion to drug trafficking and murder. His testimony shattered the Mafia's code of silence, offering a rare and unfiltered look into the inner workings of one of New York's most powerful crime families.

For the government, Gravano was a star witness whose credibility and inside knowledge made it nearly impossible for Gotti to dispute the charges against him. Gravano's cooperation also inspired other Mafia members to come forward, leading to a cascade of testimonies that helped dismantle organized crime across the country.

In court, Gravano recounted specific incidents that implicated Gotti in numerous crimes, including the murders of Paul Castellano and several other high-profile figures within the Mafia. His firsthand accounts were corroborated by FBI recordings from the Ravenite Social Club, providing a damning combination of insider knowledge and physical evidence.

The impact of Gravano's testimony was immediate and powerful; it dismantled the legal defenses that Gotti had relied on for years and undermined the mystique of invincibility that he had carefully cultivated. Gotti's lawyers struggled to counter

Gravano's revelations, and their attempts to discredit him fell short as the evidence mounted against Gotti.

For Gotti, Gravano's betrayal was a personal and professional blow. In the Mafia world, loyalty is paramount, and Gravano's defection represented the ultimate betrayal. Gotti had trusted Gravano with his life and had relied on him to help maintain control over the Gambino family. The knowledge that Gravano—a man he had once considered a brother—was now his enemy in court was a crushing realization for Gotti, marking the end of his reign and the collapse of his empire.

The betrayal also had a chilling effect on the Mafia as a whole, breaking the longstanding belief that high-ranking members would never cooperate with law enforcement. Gravano's defection shattered this illusion, creating an environment in which other mobsters began to consider turning state's evidence as a means of securing their own survival.

The repercussions of Gravano's betrayal extended far beyond Gotti's trial. His willingness to cooperate with the government set a precedent, encouraging other Mafia members to break omertà in exchange for leniency. In the years that followed, numerous high-ranking mobsters from various crime families came forward as informants, leading to an unprecedented wave of convictions and the steady decline of the Mafia's influence in New York and across the United States.

Gravano's decision to testify marked a turning point in the battle against organized crime, weakening the Mafia's grip on American cities and diminishing the power it had wielded for decades.

For John Gotti, the "Teflon Don," Gravano's betrayal marked the end of an era. The man who had once seemed untouchable was now facing a life sentence, his empire dismantled and his reputation tarnished. Gravano's testimony not only sealed Gotti's fate but also symbolized the unraveling of the Mafia's power and influence.

By breaking the Mafia's code of silence, Gravano exposed the vulnerabilities within the organization and signaled the beginning of the end for the American Mafia as it had once been known.

In the end, the bond between Gotti and Gravano—founded on loyalty, respect, and a shared commitment to the Mafia's principles—was undone by betrayal, bringing down not only Gotti himself but an entire era of organized crime.

CHAPTER EIGHT

The Downfall of the Teflon Don

John Gotti's criminal empire had survived decades of law enforcement attempts to bring it down. His skill at evading conviction had earned him the nickname "Teflon Don," a title reflecting his ability to slip through the hands of justice time and again. But in the early 1990s, his luck ran out.

After Sammy "The Bull" Gravano's defection to the government and his testimony, Gotti finally found himself facing the full force of the law. The federal government, now armed with substantial evidence, including wiretap recordings, financial records, and the testimony of insiders like Gravano, finally had the means to hold Gotti accountable for his crimes.

The trial that began in 1992 would mark the end of Gotti's reign. It was held in the United States District Court for the Eastern District of New York, a court known for handling high-profile organized crime cases. Gotti was charged with numerous offenses, including murder, racketeering, extortion, and conspiracy to commit murder.

These charges were directly linked to the operations of the Gambino family under Gotti's command, and the evidence against him seemed overwhelming. The trial was set to be one of the most significant criminal cases of the 20th century, and it would be the first time Gotti's famed "Teflon" defense would truly be tested.

The media attention surrounding the trial was intense, and the courtroom became a spectacle. Gotti, who had once thrived on the attention of the press, now found himself the center of a judicial firestorm. His public image, carefully crafted over the years as the suave, untouchable mob boss, began to fray as the details of his criminal activities became widely known. The trial was a culmination of years of investigative work and witness testimony, and it was clear that the prosecution was determined to finally put Gotti behind bars.

One of the most significant aspects of the trial was the participation of Sammy Gravano, who had turned against Gotti and become the government's star witness. Gravano's testimony would prove to be the linchpin of the prosecution's case, offering a firsthand account of the Gambino family's operations and Gotti's direct involvement in numerous murders, including the killing of Paul Castellano. Gravano's decision to testify against Gotti was a rare moment of betrayal within the Mafia, and his testimony would provide the government with the key evidence they needed to dismantle Gotti's carefully constructed defenses.

Despite his mounting legal troubles, Gotti retained his bravado. He continued to maintain his innocence, presenting himself as the victim of a coordinated effort by law enforcement to bring down a successful businessman. In court, he was defiant, attempting to project the same confident and untouchable image he had cultivated in the media. However, the more the trial progressed, the more the case against him solidified. His defense team attempted to undermine Gravano's credibility, but they struggled to counter the overwhelming weight of the evidence.

Breaking the Teflon Shield: Evidence and Testimonies Pile Up

As the trial unfolded, the prosecution systematically presented a mountain of evidence that left little room for doubt about Gotti's involvement in organized crime. The tapes made by the FBI at the Ravenite Social Club, coupled with Gravano's testimony, formed the backbone of the prosecution's case.

The wiretaps revealed Gotti's direct conversations about illegal activities, including drug trafficking, extortion, and even murder. These tapes provided irrefutable proof that Gotti was not only aware of the criminal activities taking place within his organization but was actively involved in planning and orchestrating them.

One of the most damning pieces of evidence came from the recordings of conversations where Gotti and his associates openly discussed the murder of Paul Castellano. In one of these conversations, Gotti openly acknowledges his involvement in the plot to kill Castellano, revealing his cold, calculated decision to take over the Gambino family. These revelations were a direct contradiction to Gotti's claims of innocence, exposing him as a criminal mastermind at the helm of a ruthless Mafia family.

In addition to the wiretaps, the testimony of Sammy Gravano was crucial in exposing Gotti's role in the Gambino family's activities. Gravano, once Gotti's most trusted lieutenant, described in vivid detail the inner workings of the organization, implicating Gotti in a long list of crimes. Gravano's testimony was particularly powerful because of his close relationship with Gotti.

As an insider, Gravano was able to speak with authority about Gotti's involvement in criminal activities, from extorting businesses to ordering murders. Gravano's credibility, bolstered by his firsthand

The Teflon Don

knowledge, helped to break down the protective barriers Gotti had built around himself.

The prosecution also brought in additional witnesses—former associates of Gotti who had either been arrested or turned informant—and presented documents that outlined the financial operations of the Gambino family.

These documents, which included ledgers and bank records, traced the flow of money through the family's various illegal enterprises, directly linking Gotti to the proceeds from organized crime. The combination of wiretaps, testimonies, and financial records painted a clear picture of Gotti's criminal activities, leaving little room for his defense team to refute.

112

One of the most pivotal moments in the trial came when Gotti's defense attorneys tried to discredit Gravano by suggesting that he was a liar and a self-serving criminal. However, Gravano's credibility was bolstered by the tangible evidence and corroborating testimonies, rendering these attacks on his character ineffective. The prosecution had succeeded in turning Gravano's betrayal into a powerful tool that undermined Gotti's defenses.

Guilty on All Counts: The Verdict That Shattered Gotti's Untouchable Image

On April 2, 1992, after weeks of deliberations, the jury returned with their verdict. John Gotti was found guilty on all counts, including five murders, racketeering, and a slew of other charges related to his leadership of the Gambino family. The verdict sent shockwaves through the Mafia world, marking the end of Gotti's reign as the "Teflon Don." The man who had once been considered untouchable by law enforcement was now facing the reality of a life sentence in prison, without the possibility of parole.

For Gotti, the verdict was a crushing blow. His once-mighty empire had crumbled, and the media that had once followed his every move now relished in his downfall. No longer the suave, untouchable mob boss, Gotti had become a symbol of failure. The trial had stripped away the carefully cultivated image of the Teflon Don, exposing him for the ruthless criminal he had always been. The verdict shattered the myth of

Gotti's invincibility and cemented his place in history as one of the most infamous mob bosses to ever live.

Gotti's conviction was also a major victory for law enforcement, who had spent years working tirelessly to gather the evidence needed to bring him down. The case marked a significant turning point in the FBI's battle against organized crime, proving that even the most powerful figures in the Mafia could be brought to justice.

The successful conviction of Gotti was a testament to the dedication of federal agents, the bravery of informants like Gravano, and the tireless work of prosecutors determined to dismantle the Mafia's grip on New York City.

The Teflon Don

For the American public, the conviction of John Gotti represented the end of an era. His trial had been a national spectacle, with the media covering every twist and turn. The once-feared mob boss who had commanded respect in the underworld was now facing the harsh realities of prison life. Gotti's conviction signaled the decline of the Mafia's power in New York, as his case set a precedent for the prosecution of other high-ranking Mafia members.

Though Gotti would continue to maintain his innocence even after the verdict, the evidence against him was irrefutable. His conviction had marked the end of the "Teflon Don" era, and it would signal a shift in the way organized crime in America was tackled. The government's victory over Gotti was a powerful message to other members of the Mafia—no one, not even the most untouchable, was beyond the reach of justice.

CHAPTER NINE

Life in Prison

For John Gotti, prison was a world unlike any he had experienced before. Throughout his criminal career, Gotti had carefully cultivated an image of power, invincibility, and control. On the streets, he had been the "Teflon Don"—a man above the law, who seemed untouchable, shielded from prosecution by his wealth, his network, and his ability to manipulate the system. But behind bars, Gotti faced a completely different reality.

The luxurious lifestyle he had enjoyed as the head of the Gambino family was replaced by the harsh confines of federal prison, where he had to learn to survive in a world where power was no longer defined by money or influence, but by brute strength, alliances, and the will to endure.

Gotti's transition into prison life was marked by a certain degree of denial. Though his world had drastically changed, he still clung to the illusion that he could maintain control, even behind bars. His name still carried weight within the Mafia community, and many of his former associates believed that Gotti would continue to exercise influence over the Gambino family, despite being incarcerated.

He was transferred to the United States Penitentiary at Marion, a high-security facility in Illinois, known for housing notorious criminals and organized crime figures. The prison, notorious for its strict surveillance and high-profile inmates, would become Gotti's new home for the remainder of his life.

At first, Gotti attempted to adjust to his new life by maintaining a semblance of his old persona. He was known to be a tough, defiant figure, unafraid of the threats and challenges posed by life in prison. He kept his distance from the general inmate population and primarily interacted with other Mafia figures, often giving orders to underlings through intermediaries.

But even Gotti's ability to maintain control was limited by the harsh realities of prison life. He was forced to confront the fact that, in prison, he was just another convict—vulnerable and subject to the authority of prison guards, not the powerful figures he had once commanded.

Despite his best efforts to maintain his status, Gotti's life behind bars was marked by isolation. He was placed in solitary confinement for long periods of time due to his status as a high-profile inmate and the potential threat he posed to prison security. The solitary confinement was particularly hard on Gotti, who had spent most of his life surrounded by a network of loyal associates. Now, locked away from the world, he had to adjust to the reality of being alone and vulnerable, a stark contrast to the power he had wielded outside.

Holding Onto Power: Gotti's Continued Influence from Inside

Though his physical world had shrunk to the confines of a prison cell, John Gotti was determined to hold onto whatever power and influence he had left. For years, he had been the undisputed boss of the Gambino family, and he believed that he could still control the family's operations, even from prison.

Gotti maintained a carefully orchestrated network of intermediaries, including his son John Gotti Jr., who would become the family's titular leader in his absence. Gotti's influence was not limited to his biological family; many of his loyal associates on the outside continued to consult with him and follow his orders, treating him as the de facto head of the Gambino family.

From his prison cell, Gotti was able to maintain communication with the outside world. Despite being confined to solitary for a large part of his sentence, he managed to use the phone system, mail, and his family connections to stay involved in the Mafia's affairs. Gotti's son John Gotti Jr. was instrumental in carrying out his father's wishes, and many of the Gambino family's activities continued under the younger Gotti's direction, all while John Sr. remained the boss in name, if not in reality.

Gotti's ability to maintain this level of control in the face of such adversity was a testament to his will and determination. He understood the inner workings of the Mafia better than anyone and was able to leverage his remaining power and connections to exert influence over his family's operations. While he could no longer make public appearances or direct meetings with the same hands-on approach he had used on the outside, he still wielded considerable power through his underlings. Even from behind bars, Gotti's reputation as a ruthless and cunning leader continued to resonate in the criminal world.

However, as Gotti's time in prison wore on, his efforts to maintain his grip on the family became increasingly difficult. His isolation, the constant surveillance, and his limited ability to communicate with the outside world took a toll on his capacity to control the Gambino family. Though his son John

Jr. and loyal associates did their best to keep his legacy alive, the family's operations slowly began to shift, and Gotti's direct influence began to wane. The emergence of new players in the Mafia scene and the constant pressure from law enforcement made it harder for Gotti to retain the level of control he had once enjoyed.

The Slow Decline: Gotti's Health Worsens and Control Fades

As the years passed, John Gotti's physical health began to deteriorate. He had always been a man of considerable physical presence, a key part of his image as a tough, untouchable figure. But now, the man who had once been able to control a criminal empire from the streets was increasingly confined to a hospital bed. Gotti was diagnosed with throat cancer in the mid-1990s, and his health began to decline rapidly. The disease weakened him physically and emotionally, leaving him more vulnerable than he had ever been.

In prison, Gotti's once-commanding presence faded as he became more and more dependent on medical care. He underwent various treatments, including radiation and chemotherapy, but his condition worsened over time. The cancer took a severe toll on his ability to speak and breathe, a cruel irony for a man who had spent so much of his life commanding respect through his voice and his demeanor. Gotti's once vibrant personality began to fade, replaced by the grim reality of his own mortality.

Gotti's health issues further complicated his ability to maintain control over the Gambino family. His family and associates, particularly his son John Jr., continued to carry out his wishes, but without Gotti's direct involvement, the family slowly shifted toward a more decentralized structure. Other members of the Mafia, sensing the weakening of Gotti's control, began to assert their own influence within the Gambino family. The once-unified front that Gotti had maintained began to crack, and by the time of his death, Gotti's influence had significantly diminished.

In 2002, after battling throat cancer for several years, John Gotti passed away in prison at the age of 61. His death marked the final chapter of a life filled with power, infamy, and the constant struggle to maintain control. Though Gotti's empire had already begun to unravel by the time of his death, his legacy lived on in the lore of organized crime and the stories of his rise and fall. His ability to elude conviction for so long, his brazen style, and his ruthless pursuit of power made him a legend in the criminal world, even as his health declined and his control faded.

Gotti's passing represented the end of an era for the Gambino family and for the Mafia in New York City. His son, John Gotti Jr., would eventually take over the family business, but the days of the Mafia as a dominant force in American society were fading.

The power structures that Gotti had once controlled with an iron fist were gradually being replaced by new, more modern criminal enterprises. Though Gotti's death closed the door on his personal reign, the legend of the "Teflon Don" continued to haunt the criminal world, a reminder of a time when one man could hold so much power, even in the face of seemingly insurmountable odds.

CHAPTER TEN

Legacy and Infamy

John Gotti's death in 2002 marked more than just the passing of an infamous criminal mastermind; it symbolized the end of an era for the Mafia in New York and the United States. His passing brought to a close one of the most spectacular and dramatic careers in organized crime history.

Gotti had spent decades at the top of the criminal underworld, running the Gambino family with absolute authority, commanding respect through fear, and evading law enforcement's best efforts to put him behind bars.

His death in prison from throat cancer came after years of decline, both personally and within the Gambino family. During the last decade of his life, the power and influence of the Mafia had begun to wane significantly. Law enforcement had stepped up its efforts against organized crime, and the federal government had begun to dismantle the Mafia families through a combination of legal and undercover operations, along with the cooperation of former Mafia insiders, such as Sammy Gravano.

Gotti's absence from the street didn't cause an immediate collapse of the Gambino family, but it did represent a clear break in the way things had operated for decades. Under his leadership, the Gambino family had been one of the most powerful and feared criminal organizations in the world, with a reach extending across New York, the

U.S., and even internationally. Gotti's strategic brilliance, his ability to outmaneuver law enforcement, and his unwavering commitment to the code of the Mafia had made him the epitome of Mafia leadership.

However, in the years following his death, the Gambino family, like all Mafia organizations, began to experience significant challenges. Internal power struggles, heightened law enforcement pressure, and the rise of non-Mafia organized crime groups weakened traditional Mafia power.

Younger, more entrepreneurial crime figures, often involved in cybercrime or other illicit businesses, began to replace the old guard. Gotti's son, John Gotti Jr., briefly tried to take control, but without the same charismatic leadership and the resources his father had once commanded, the Gambino family struggled to maintain its former dominance.

Moreover, the shifting political and social landscape in New York—coupled with the changing nature of crime—meant that the Mafia was no longer the dominant criminal force it had once been. The decline of traditional organized crime coincided with the rise of other illegal activities such as cybercrime, identity theft, and the global drug trade, which were more difficult to infiltrate and take down with traditional methods.

Though Gotti's death did not immediately spell the end of the Gambino family, it certainly marked the conclusion of an era where the Mafia had been a pervasive and powerful institution in American society. His passing signified the fading of the once-legendary criminal organizations that had ruled New York and other major cities for much of the 20th century. While his death may not have entirely dissolved the Mafia, it certainly marked a significant turning point in its history.

The Media and Pop Culture Icon: How Gotti Became a Symbol

In death, John Gotti became something far more enduring than just a mob boss; he became a symbol. His life, particularly his rise to prominence within the Gambino family, was laden with intrigue, charisma, and violent drama, which naturally captivated the public's imagination.

From the moment he was dubbed the "Teflon Don" by the media due to his uncanny ability to avoid conviction, Gotti became a fixture in the headlines, making him a subject of both fascination and revulsion. But it was his death that solidified his place in pop culture as one of the most infamous figures in American history.

Gotti's larger-than-life persona, cultivated through his public appearances, his media savvy, and his audacious defiance of the law, made him the ultimate "antihero" in the eyes of the public. He played to the press, often inviting journalists into his world and enjoying the spotlight they provided.

His sharp suits, his smooth talk, and his confident, sometimes cocky demeanor turned him into a kind of Mafia celebrity. At the height of his power, he was a mob boss who seemed untouchable, walking the streets of New York with the same swagger as a Hollywood star.

In the years following his death, Gotti's image was immortalized in movies, television shows, and documentaries. The 1996 TV movie *Gotti*, starring Armand Assante, and later the 2018 biopic *Gotti*, starring John Travolta, portrayed the complexities of his rise to power, his defiance of the law, and his role in the Mafia underworld.

These depictions, though often dramatized, helped shape the narrative of Gotti's life, portraying him as both a ruthless crime boss and a charming, charismatic figure—a man who, despite his violent tendencies, maintained a sense of honor and loyalty within his own family.

Gotti's story became a rich source for countless books, films, and television programs, all of which contributed to the mythology surrounding his life. In many of these portrayals, Gotti was cast as a tragic figure, someone whose brilliant criminal mind was ultimately his undoing.

His ability to manipulate the press, his unshakable confidence, and his ultimate fall from grace made him a fascinating subject for both the media and the public, ensuring his place in the pantheon of famous mobsters, alongside figures like Al Capone and Lucky Luciano.

But Gotti's influence on popular culture went beyond film and television. His name and likeness have been used in songs, books, and even political discourse. In some circles, particularly in the realm of hip-hop, Gotti was adopted as an icon of rebellion, a symbol of power and success in the face of authority. His image—immortalized in photographs of him in his sharp suits, a cigar in hand—became emblematic of the allure of the criminal world, a world that, despite its dangers, seemed to offer a path to power and respect.

The myth of the "Teflon Don" became larger than life, creating a legacy that transcended the criminal underworld and embedded itself in American pop culture. John Gotti was no longer just a mob boss—he was a symbol of defiance, a complex character who straddled the line between hero and villain, lawbreaker and leader. And as much as law enforcement worked to dismantle the Mafia, Gotti's celebrity status and his role in the public consciousness ensured that his legacy would continue to live on, albeit in a different form than he might have imagined.

The Teflon Don's Lasting Influence: The Myth and Reality of John Gotti

John Gotti's lasting influence is perhaps most evident in the myth that has surrounded him. The "Teflon Don" moniker, which once signified his miraculous ability to avoid conviction, has become a part of the folklore surrounding his life.

Even today, nearly two decades after his death, Gotti's name remains synonymous with both the Mafia and the media's portrayal of organized crime. His story is both a cautionary tale of power and corruption and a reflection of the allure of the Mafia lifestyle that still resonates in American culture.

Gotti's life and legacy continue to be debated. For some, he is a tragic figure, a man whose rise to power was marked by incredible ambition, but whose eventual downfall serves as a reminder of the dangers of hubris. His ability to avoid conviction for years, coupled with his brazen public image, made him a legend in the criminal world. In many respects, he was the last of the great Mafia bosses—the last to hold the kind of undeniable influence that had defined organized crime for much of the 20th century.

But there is also a darker side to Gotti's legacy. While he was admired for his cunning and his ability to evade the law, he was also responsible for heinous acts of violence and murder. His control over the Gambino family was built on a foundation of fear and brutality, and his reign led to the deaths of countless individuals, many of whom were caught in the crossfire of his violent ascent to power.

Gotti's association with organized crime—particularly the notorious hits, such as the murder of Paul Castellano—remains a stain on his legacy that no amount of media coverage can erase.

The reality of John Gotti's life, while often romanticized in media portrayals, is far more complex than the myth that surrounds him. His story is not just one of Mafia power and defiance of the law but also one of betrayal, manipulation, and the inevitable decline that comes with living a life rooted in crime. His eventual conviction, betrayal by Sammy Gravano, and ultimate death in prison serve as stark reminders of the price of a life led by violence and crime.

In the end, Gotti's legacy is a double-edged sword. While his rise to power and his notorious public persona have become iconic, the true reality of his actions remains a cautionary tale. The myth of the Teflon Don may continue to captivate the public's imagination, but the reality is far more tragic—a man whose legacy was ultimately defined not by his success, but by his violent methods, his betrayal of those closest to him, and the inevitable consequences of living outside the law.

CONCLUSION

The Rise and Fall of John Gotti: Summing Up a Life of Crime and Consequence

John Gotti's life was marked by extremes: a meteoric rise to power in the criminal underworld and a catastrophic fall that shattered the myth of the "Teflon Don." Born into poverty in the working-class neighborhoods of the Bronx, Gotti's ascent to the top of the Gambino family epitomized the American underworld's darkest dreams—a tale of ambition, ruthlessness, and an unwavering will to dominate.

Throughout his career, Gotti defied law enforcement at every turn, managing to evade conviction for multiple heinous crimes, thanks to his manipulation of the justice system, his network of loyal associates, and his flair for the dramatic. His "Teflon Don" persona became synonymous with invincibility, and for many, he represented the embodiment of the Mafia's power and glory.

However, Gotti's downfall was as dramatic as his rise. After years of evading the law, his empire came crashing down when Sammy "The Bull" Gravano, his trusted confidant, turned against him. This betrayal was the final blow to Gotti's power, culminating in his conviction on charges that included murder and racketeering.

Despite his status as one of the most notorious figures in the criminal world, Gotti could not escape the consequences of his violent lifestyle. His story is a poignant reminder of the inevitable costs of living outside the law—no matter how powerful or untouchable one might appear.

Gotti's fall from grace was not just the result of betrayal, but also the culmination of decades of violence, manipulation, and greed. His arrogance and the belief that he could control his fate, even behind bars, only delayed the inevitable. In the end, Gotti's story is one of a man who sought to defy the very forces that shaped his existence, only to be consumed by them.

His ultimate demise—dying in prison from cancer after years of deterioration—was both tragic and fitting for a figure who lived his life as though he were above reproach, only to be humbled by time, law enforcement, and his own mortality.

The Shattered Image: Lessons from the Teflon Don's Reign and Demise

John Gotti's reign and eventual demise offer several powerful lessons that resonate far beyond the world of organized crime. One of the most poignant lessons is the fragile nature of power and the illusion of invincibility. For much of his life, Gotti appeared untouchable—his ability to dodge convictions and rise to the top of the Mafia hierarchy made him seem impervious to the forces of justice and law.

Yet, as history has shown, no amount of power, wealth, or influence can ultimately protect a person from the consequences of their actions. Gotti's life was built on violence, betrayal, and manipulation, and these same forces ultimately led to his downfall.

Another lesson from Gotti's story is the impact of loyalty and betrayal in the Mafia world. Throughout his rise to power, Gotti relied heavily on loyal associates, including Sammy Gravano, who once considered Gotti a mentor and friend.

When Gravano ultimately turned on him, his betrayal not only marked the end of Gotti's criminal reign but also highlighted the fragility of trust within criminal organizations. In the Mafia, loyalty is paramount, but the treacherous nature of organized crime means that even the most trusted figures can be swayed by self-interest or the promise of leniency.

Perhaps the most significant lesson from Gotti's story is the inevitability of consequence. The Mafia's violent world may reward cunning, brutality, and ruthlessness, but those who operate within it cannot escape the eventual repercussions of their actions. Gotti's life is a cautionary tale about the toll that a life of crime can take—on one's family, one's freedom, and one's soul.

Though Gotti's image as the "Teflon Don" remains etched in the public's consciousness, the reality of his life is a tragic reminder that, in the end, no one is truly above the law or above the consequences of their actions.

A Lasting Legacy: The Enduring Fascination with the Mafia and Gotti

Despite his death and the subsequent decline of the Mafia's power, John Gotti's legacy endures. His story, filled with intrigue, violence, and audacity, has become the stuff of legend, influencing popular culture and continuing to captivate the public's imagination.

Gotti was not only the last great Mafia boss to dominate the streets of New York but also a figure who personified the allure of the criminal world. His rise to power, his defiance of authority, and his ultimate downfall have become a symbol of both the promise and the perils of a life lived on the edge.

The Teflon Don

Gotti's influence on pop culture cannot be overstated. His story has been immortalized in films, books, and television series, where his larger-than-life persona continues to capture the attention of audiences around the world. He has been portrayed as everything from a charming antihero to a tragic figure, embodying the timeless conflict between power and consequence. The phrase "Teflon Don" has entered the public lexicon as shorthand for someone who is seemingly immune to prosecution, cementing Gotti's place as a cultural icon of the criminal world.

Beyond the media portrayals, Gotti's legacy also lives on through the lessons learned from his rise and fall. His life serves as a stark reminder of the dangers of living outside the law, the consequences of betrayal, and the ultimate price of ambition unchecked by morality. In the years since his death, his story has continued to fascinate those who are drawn to the complex world of organized crime and the individuals who inhabit it.

For many, Gotti remains an emblematic figure of the Mafia's golden age—an era that, though fading, still holds a certain mystique in American culture. His ability to manipulate the media, his charisma, and his ruthless ambition made him the last true figurehead of the traditional Mafia. As the world has moved on and the criminal underworld has evolved, Gotti's name continues to resonate as the symbol of a bygone era when the Mafia reigned supreme.

Even though the Mafia has long since lost its stranglehold on organized crime, Gotti's story endures as a reflection of a time when the world of organized crime was more visible, more audacious, and more feared. His legacy is not one of redemption or triumph, but rather one of myth, mythologized by the media, the public, and the Mafia itself.

The "Teflon Don" may have been brought down by the very forces he thought he could control, but in death, he remains an indelible figure in the pantheon of America's most notorious criminals.

THANKS FOR READING!!!

Milton Keynes UK
Ingram Content Group UK Ltd.
UKHW020704021224
3298UKWH00039B/367

9 798330 587995